I am me

&

I MAKE A DIFFERENCE

**Awesome Stories of Big Hearts and Bold Dreams
By a Group of Amazing Young Authors**

I AM ME & I MAKE A DIFFERENCE

Contents

Foreword: The Power of a Young Heart and Mind

Welcome to a book unlike any other—a collection of voices that are young in age but immense in spirit. I AM ME & I MAKE A DIFFERENCE: Awesome Stories of Big Hearts and Bold Dreams is more than just a collection of texts; it is a profound declaration by a new generation.

Each chapter begins with a child's handwritten or spoken response to a series of reflective questions designed to spark self-discovery and creativity. Our young authors poured their thoughts and feelings into their drafts, and our editorial team carefully helped them organize their ideas into cohesive chapters—without changing their authentic voices. To ensure accessibility for all readers, the stories were translated into either Farsi or English based on each child's mother tongue. While modern AI tools were used to support editing and translation, the heart and originality of this book lie entirely in the children's genuine answers and authentic expressions, carefully led by our team of experts.

To our young authors: you have done something courageous. It takes true courage to share your innermost thoughts, your biggest dreams, and your deepest hopes with the world. Through your words, you teach us that a four-year-old can be an artist who thinks about nature, a nine-year-old can show us the superpower of kindness, and a twelve-year-old can see the world through the lens of boundless creativity, all while prioritizing peace. You remind us that a bright future doesn't wait for grown-ups; it begins right now, with every thoughtful question, every act of kindness, and every creative idea.

This book is a symbol of diversity, hope, and the incredible potential that lives within every child. Each author brings their unique light, showing us the beauty of different passions—from coding and Taekwondo to drawing, grand piano performance, and the simple joy of imaginary books. These stories illustrate a fundamental truth: no matter our age, background, or interests, we are all connected by the desire to make the world a better, kinder, and fairer place.

To the parents who helped these voices shine: thank you. The supportive words that follow each child's chapter are a testament to your unconditional love and guidance. It is in homes filled with curiosity, encouragement, and the freedom to dream big that great people are raised. You have nurtured thinkers, creators, and helpers, and in doing so, you have given this book—and the world—a tremendous gift.

As you turn these pages, prepare to be inspired. You will find that the biggest dreams often reside in the youngest hearts. May the stories within encourage you, no matter your age, to find your voice, believe in your power to make a difference, and boldly declare: "I Am Me & I Make a Difference."

Dr. Katayoon Bidad
Co-founder of North Star Success Publishing Company

Aiden's World

I'm Aiden, and I Think about Big Things

My name is Aiden Anari. I'm seven years old, and I live in the big city of Toronto.
I'm brave and creative, and I think a lot. My parents say I was born asking "why."
Even when I was really little, I asked big questions like, what if this is all a dream
and one day we wake up somewhere else?
Or what happens after we die? Can we become plants,
animals, or even be present in the skies, overlooking the earth?
These thoughts don't make me sad, they make me curious.

My Brother and Me

My brother and I are a great team. We play, laugh, and create together, especially when it comes to our imaginary world, Spakia. Spakia is a country I created years ago. It's not on any map, but in our minds, it's as real as Earth! My brother is the King, and I'm the Prime Minister.
We even made up our own language, Spaken, and we sometimes speak it, and no one else understands. In Spakia, there are no wars, no pollution, and no wasting energy. Everyone lives in peace and helps each other.

Energy Is Important

I really care about saving energy. I don't like wasting electricity, water, or anything that comes from nature. Whenever I leave a room, I turn off the lights, even if I'm coming back soon. I remind my family that small actions matter. If every person saved a little energy every day, the whole world would be better off. I want people to understand that taking care of the Earth isn't just about trees or animals, it's about respecting the energy that keeps everything alive. I sometimes imagine Spakia running completely on clean energy, powered by sunlight, wind, and water. No smoke, no waste, just smart people working together for the future.

My Games and Creations

I love video games but not just playing them, I like creating them too!
I invented my own game called Fartarn. It's funny, clever, and full of challenges.
In Fartarn, you must use logic and creativity to navigate levels while maintaining
a clean and balanced world.

When I play with my brother, we often discuss ways to improve the game,
such as making the rules smarter or designing new characters.
We love creating together because it feels like we're building something big,
something that could make people smile and think..

My Big Dreams

I have a lot of dreams for the future. One of them is to become a billionaire, not just to be rich, but so I can help people. I want to build hospitals and shelters for those who need them. I'd also love to fund big inventions that can make the world a more peaceful and fair place. I want to be someone who uses money for good things, like developing clean energy, creating smart machines that help with hard jobs, and supporting people who don't have homes. My dream is to make life easier and happier for everyone. I have even started to make a homework machine for kids to do their homework for them!

I'm Aiden, big thoughts and with my and imagination, I want to make a world where everyone is smart and happy.

Aiden surprises us every day with how deeply he thinks about
the world. He looks at everything from a different angle, always
asking "why?" and trying to understand the meaning behind things.
We often call him our little philosopher because he asks big questions,
about life, creation, death, and even peace. He never accepts simple
answers and always wants to understand things fully.
He's also brilliant, curious, and creative. Aiden loves reading, coding,
and practicing Taekwondo. His imagination shines through
when he reads or listens to stories like Harry Potter, he gets so excited
about the characters and the worlds they live in that he even asks us to
email his favorite authors to tell them to write more books!
Aiden is generous in the truest sense. He shares what he has and what he
loves, whether it's a toy, a snack, or an idea. He often talks with his
brother about Fartarn, the game he created in his imagination,
and about what makes a good gamer. Sometimes, in the middle of
their conversations, he'll say something like, "Make a decision that's
better for your future," and we can't help but smile.
He sounds wise beyond his years. We love how Aiden's mind is always
full of questions, creativity, and kindness. He reminds us that
deep thinking and a caring heart can live beautifully in
one small, thoughtful boy.

My Family Says...

Kason's World

I'm Kason, and I Bring Joy to Everything!

Hi! My name is Kason Anari, and I'm nine years old. I live in the big, exciting city of Toronto, Canada, with my family. Everyone knows me by my voice, and of course, my always messy room!
I love doing group activities with my family and friends, playing games, drawing together, or playing basketball in the park. I'm really good at riding my bike, ice-skating, and playing Roblox, and I love making people laugh. I think laughter is like sunshine, it makes everything brighter.

What I Love Most Is Kindness

When I'm outside, I feel happy and free. I love going for walks or runs,
watching animals, and playing with my brother and friends.
One cold winter day, my brother and I were ice skating. He suddenly fell
and hurt his knee. Without even thinking, I ran to help him up.
In that moment, I felt something strong inside me, like kindness could make
the wholeworld warmer. Since then, I've promised myself always to help others,
especially people who have no homes and must sleep outside.
I wish everyone could have a warm place to stay.

Me and My World

I really love the Earth and the world I live in. If I see trash on the ground,
I don't walk past it, I pick it up. I want to make parks, schools, and neighborhoods
cleaner and better for everyone.
But here's a secret: my friends and I have a super cool plan.
We want to invent Utron! Utron is a magical crystal, a guardian of
the Earth that stops trash from harming the planet.
I even dream of building a machine that turns trash into useful things before it even
touches the ground! Maybe one day, it will be real.

My Big Dreams

Sometimes, I wish I had a time machine to travel to the past or future.
I'd love to see how my grandpa played as a kid, or meet my future self as
a grown-up entrepreneur. I have big dreams. When I grow up, I want to
own my own business, something creative that helps people
and the planet at the same time. I want to be strong, confident, and kind.
No matter how much power I have, I'll use it to make the world a better place.
If I had a superpower, it would be the power of kindness. I think kindness
is stronger than anything, stronger than anger, stronger than fear.

Little Moments
That Make Me Smile

Honestly, I don't love being in photos, I'd rather be the one taking them.
But before I take a picture of others, I always sneak in a funny selfie first!
Once, during a Nowruz celebration, I won a prize. A little boy nearby
looked sad because he didn't win anything. I secretly gave him my prize.
Nobody noticed, but my heart felt super happy.
I also play chess and practice reading Farsi. When I win my dad in chess
or read a Farsi story out loud, my parents look at me with so much pride,
it makes me want to keep learning more.

I'm Kason, and with my kindness,
curiosity, and big dreams, I hope to make
the world a brighter place.

Kason is bright, kind, imaginative, and very social. He fills
our home with laughter and ideas. From a young age, he has
shown deep empathy for others and a natural curiosity about
how the world works.
He always cares about others and is thoughtful, whether it's
looking out for his younger brother, cheering up a friend, or
spending quality time with family and friends. He loves thinking
about and creating games, using his imagination to make
playtime fun and exciting for everyone.
He's wonderfully active and approaches everything he does
with focus and determination, usually becoming really good
at whatever he sets his mind on. His creativity shines
through his drawings, storytelling, and games.
What we love most about Kason is his big heart. Whether he's
spending time with friends, exploring new activities, or simply
making others laugh, he does everything with kindness and joy.
We believe he will grow into someone who makes
the world a better place.

My Family Says...

Radin's World

I'm Radin, and I Love Creating and Discovering!

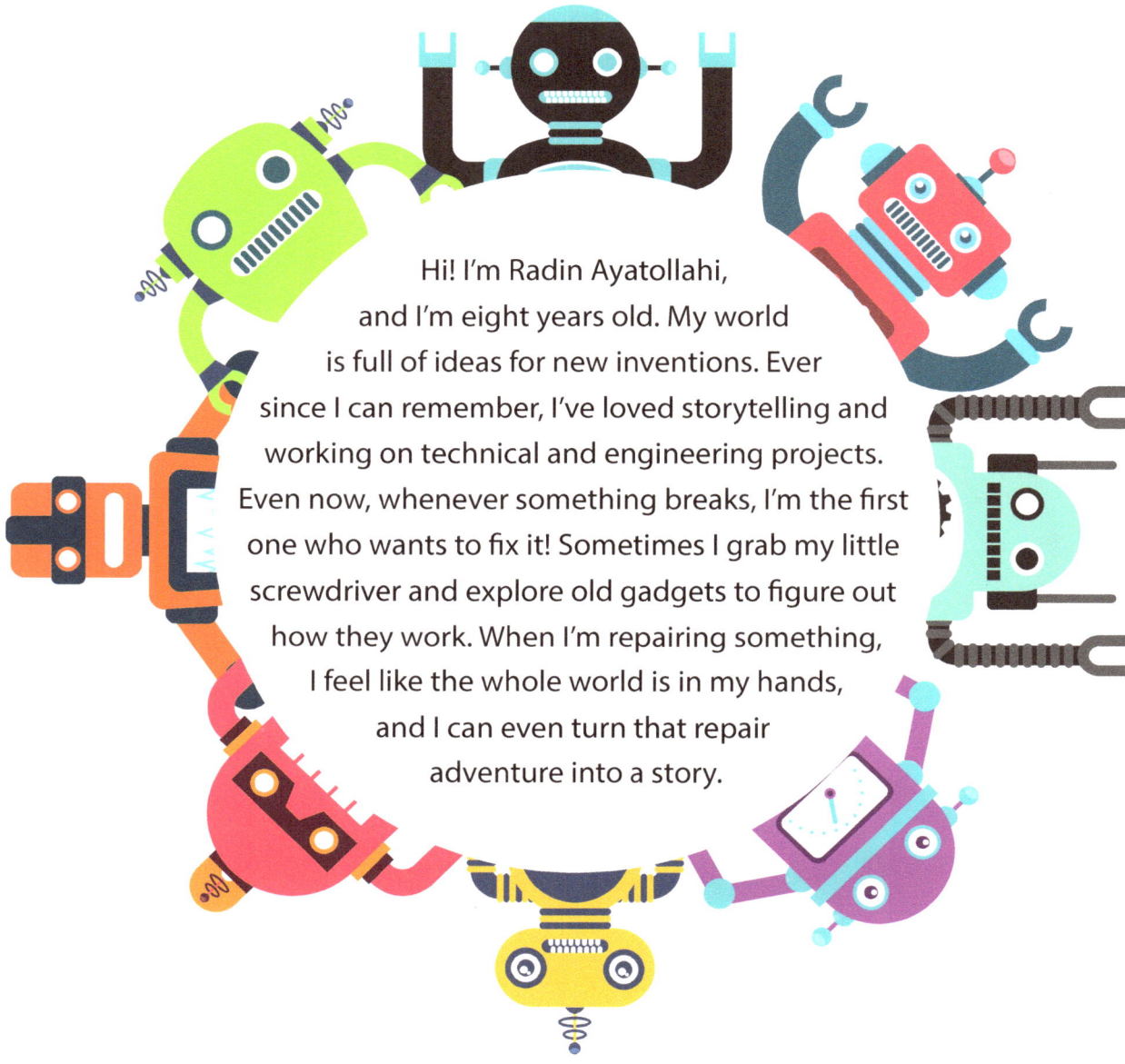

Hi! I'm Radin Ayatollahi, and I'm eight years old. My world is full of ideas for new inventions. Ever since I can remember, I've loved storytelling and working on technical and engineering projects. Even now, whenever something breaks, I'm the first one who wants to fix it! Sometimes I grab my little screwdriver and explore old gadgets to figure out how they work. When I'm repairing something, I feel like the whole world is in my hands, and I can even turn that repair adventure into a story.

My friends and teachers say I'm really good at math, Persian, and especially programming with Scratch. They even think I could teach programming and robotics to others. I love solving problems and building new things; for example, every time I create something new in Scratch, it feels like I've invented something amazing!

The Best Moments of My Life

In addition to surprise birthday parties, the best moments of my life are when I splash around and go to the water park with my dad, or play PS5, eat ice cream, and watch cartoons with my mom. At those times, it feels like nothing in the world could be better! Since I was little, I've loved trying everything, from frying eggs to writing, building robots, and traveling around the world. Writing used to be hard for me, but now I'm really good at it. Sometimes I even help my teachers at school and assist them during recess. Doing this always makes me feel happy.

Kindness and Helping Others

I care deeply about kindness and helping others. For example, I always try to
share my snacks with my friends, and if they're feeling down, I play with them
to lift their mood. At home, I always help out too: I wash dishes and fruit, cook rice,
and assist my dad with technical projects. I believe kindness is more than just
a feeling; it must be shown through actions. I also love nature. I don't like it when anyone
litters or harms animals. Sometimes I even wish I could make medicine taste better
so sick people could take it more easily!
Nature, animals, and health are very important to me. Life itself, and living it well,
is more valuable than anything else.

My Big Dreams

When I think about the future, I want to have two jobs: engineer and animator.
Through engineering, I can design innovative solutions and contribute to
the world's advancement, while animation allows me to bring joy to the world.
One of my dreams is to build robots that do hard work, so people don't get so tired.
For example, a robot that cleans the streets and protects nature.
I think if everyone learns not to litter and keeps the water clean,
our planet will always stay beautiful!
If I were a superhero, my name would be "Radin the All-Smart Master"!
Then I could put out fires with a snap of my fingers, fly through the sky,
and fix any broken gadget just by touching it!
I would go anywhere, but only on Earth, because it is my home. I would help
the trees, animals, and people wherever I went. If I were a superhero, I would always
take my grandma, grandpa, mom, and dad on my heroic adventures, because
they are the ones who give me my power. Together, we would travel to
places where nature had been damaged and help repair it. I think that if everyone
had the power to help others, the world would become a much better place.

In short, I am Radin: a boy who loves creating, discovering, helping, and being kind. Every day, I'm learning how to use my mind, creativity, and kind heart to make the world a little better than it was yesterday.

Radin is a creative, kind, and careful boy. His mind is always busy, discovering things; from figuring out how different gadgets work to thinking about how he can invent something new. When Radin repairs a device or carefully retells the details of a story, it shows how much attention he pays to the most minor things. Along with his curiosity, Radin's independence is remarkable. He usually tries to find solutions on his own rather than waiting for others. One moment we will never forget is the day a little sparrow sat on a branch of a grapevine, eating grapes. When Radin saw the bird as he was passing by, he quietly changed his path so it wouldn't get scared and could continue eating. That simple gesture revealed the kindness in his heart. Another memory of Radin comes from a school trip to the water park. That day, Radin missed the school bus, and the teacher didn't notice he wasn't there. Instead of panicking or crying, Radin went to the park staff himself and asked them to contact us. He handled the situation calmly and responsibly, leaving everyone amazed. That day, we felt prouder than ever of our son's maturity and confidence.

My Family Says...

Lena's World

I'm Lena, and I Love Learning!

Hi!

I'm Lena Deihimi, eight years old, kind, and passionate about nature and learning. I enjoy creating, imagining, and trying new things. Whether I'm practicing Taekwondo, writing stories, or pretending to be a teacher for my toys, I put my whole heart into it.

I speak three languages, Farsi, English, and French, and I think stories have the power to change the world.

I also believe kindness can, too.

I'm One with Nature

That's how I would describe myself. I love being outside, feeling the sun, watching animals, and singing softly as I walk through the world.
I even created an imaginary pet named Mak Mak, who became so popular that my friends and teachers all wanted to hear about its adventures.
Nature is important to me, just like kindness, fairness, and friendship.
I believe I'm important to myself, and that's something everyone should feel.
I'm proud of who I am and who I'm becoming.

I Love Taekwandoo

I love Taekwondo. I started as a beginner, and now
I've worked so hard that I've become really good at it.
It makes me proud because it shows me what I can
do when I don't give up.

I also Love Teaching!

One of my favorite things to do is create a pretend school or daycare for my dolls, my toys, or even my parents. I act like the teacher and teach them the alphabet, painting, or whatever fun lesson I can think of. It makes me feel excited and creative. Drawing and painting are also some of my favorite things. When I write books, I even illustrate them myself. Recently, I've been learning to draw characters based on their personalities. It's like bringing their stories to life.

In My Own Little Lab

I also love science, and sometimes I play scientist in my own little lab, doing experiments with excitement and curiosity.
And video games?
I could play them all day. They're like magical worlds where you can explore, discover, and be someone new.
I love that feeling of adventure.

I'm Proud of...

I'm proud of how far I've come. Learning to skate was challenging at first, but now I'm quite skilled at it. My teacher even says I look professional! She told my mom to get me special skates so I can join races. That made me feel really proud.

I'm also proud of my reading and writing. My teachers and friends say I'm amazing at it, and when I was in senior kindergarten, my teacher said I could read like someone in grade five. I even want to teach others how to write their own stories, because I believe everyone has something special to say.

One of my proudest moments was playing piano on stage in front of more than 50 people when I was only five. It was the first time I touched a grand piano, and I performed with joy and confidence.

My Words for The World!

There's something important I want to share with you.
Being a good friend means letting others make their own
choices and being kind. That's what I try to do every day.
I care deeply about kindness, fairness, and helping others.
Once, at Canada's Wonderland, my friend and I saw a squirrel
that looked really hot. We gave it water because we wanted to help.
That moment reminded me that even small acts of kindness can make
a big difference. I also believe in listening, especially to the people I love,
like my parents. I want to understand them and be there for them,
just like they are for me. If I could teach the world one lesson,
it would be to be more understanding.

I am Lena and
I believe that if we all tried just
a little harder to listen and
understand one another, the world
would be a much better place.

From the very beginning, Lena has amazed us with
her creativity, kindness, and curiosity.
She could read fluently at the age of four and has since
picked up multiple languages, sometimes in the most surprising ways,
like translating Spanish after a trip to Cuba, just by listening and
noticing the colors on a box of crayons.
She has a natural talent for storytelling, often writing and illustrating
her own books, each one more thoughtful and imaginative than the last.
Whether she's building games out of recycled materials, painting Nowruz scenes
that get displayed at cultural events, or inventing video game-style
characters with shape-based personalities, her artistic mind is always buzzing.
But it's her heart that makes her truly special.
Once, without being asked, she helped a new classmate who had just
moved from Iran feel welcomed and supported, something we only
found out later from a proud teacher.
At home, Lena fills our days with joyful stories, nightly talks, and gentle
reminders that every creature deserves kindness, even no matter how small,
like the tiniest bug in the house.
She's a leader among her friends, a quiet helper at school, and someone
who carries her cultural pride with joy. We once found her, at the age
of two, trying to "save" a giant dead mouse on a farm while holding it
in her tiny hands. That moment, strange and sweet, said it all:
Lena's love for all living things is as real as it gets.

My Family Says...

Avan's World

I'm Avan, and I Paint My World with Music and Color!

Hi! My name is Avan Ghasemipoor, and I'm eight years old.
My world is full of color, music, and kindness. I really love painting because it lets me bring to life all the things I dream of doing and capture them on paper.
I also love swimming in the sea or in the pool under the sunlight, listening to the music of the water as I move.

Volleyball is my favorite sport, and when I manage to land the ball perfectly on the other team's side and my team wins, my heart beats fast with excitement. My coach always encourages me, saying I'm a cheerful and energetic player.

My Skills and What I've Learned

I'm good at math and spelling. My teacher says I have an organized mind and work carefully. I also play the violin. Initially, I found playing the violin challenging because I had to focus on both the notes and the bow simultaneously. But now, when I play, I feel like the sound of the violin becomes one with the sound of my heart. Sometimes, after practice, I play for my family, and when I see their smiles, I'm sure that music can make people happy. Riding my bike feels like flying! When I pedal and the wind blows through my hair, it feels as if I'm moving across the clouds. Sometimes I go to the park and ride so much that I get tired, but I still don't want to go home!

Kindness and Friendship

I believe that being a good friend means being kind and staying by your friend's side, even when things get difficult. I try to share my stuff with my friends, draw pictures for them, or help them with math. When I see someone feeling sad, I sit next to them and talk until they feel better. If someone falls or forgets something, I help them; I can't ignore it. I want everyone around me to feel safe and happy.

I love animals too, because they have feelings just like we do. When I see a cat, I smile at it and, if I can, I gently pet it. Nature is also critical to me. I always remind my mom that we should never litter, so our planet stays clean, and the flowers can thrive!

Making a Difference at Home and School

At home, I like to help keep everything tidy: I set the lunch table, arrange the glasses, and bring water for my mom when she's tired. I also give my dad a massage and sometimes bring him his special pillow so he can rest more comfortably. I love seeing their smiles, knowing that my small actions bring great happiness to their hearts.

At school, I also try to be helpful. For example, if a friend doesn't have a pencil, I lend them one, or if someone doesn't understand a math problem, I explain it until they do. Sometimes my teacher asks me to help the younger students, and that always makes me very happy.

My Big Dreams

I have a big dream. When I grow up, I want to become President so that I can help people. I want to make a law that allows all children in the world to go to school and protects all animals from harm. I also want to invent things that make people's lives easier and help keep the Earth free from pollution. Sometimes I imagine that if I were a superhero, I could fly, open doors with my mind, and clean the whole Earth of garbage with just one gesture. If I had that power, I would travel with my mom, dad, and my sister, Baran, setting all the zoo animals free. I want the world to be a kinder place, a place where people help each other and smile more.

Avan means freshness and life, and being Avan means being kind, smiling, and helping others. I am Avan, a girl who wants to make the world brighter with painting, music, and kindness. I hope that one day, with my violin or my words, I can bring happiness to everyone's heart.

Avan is a determined, kind, and energetic girl. Whatever she starts,
she continues with patience and focus until she reaches her goal.
Through consistent practice, she has made remarkable progress
in learning the violin. When she swims, she dives deep
into the water with confidence and determination, showing
no trace of fear in her eyes.

Avan has a gentle yet strong spirit. Even as a child, she was
curious and loved to talk with us, and still today, her answers are
always thoughtful and reflective.

At home, her presence is full of love and care.
When her sister was sick, Avan took care of her and helped
with everything she needed. Another fond memory of hers is the day
she made milkshakes to cheer us up. At school, too, Avan brightens
those around her with her friendly behavior and cheerful words.

The night we saw her performing at the music concert in
Niavaran Cultural Center, calm and in harmony among the other
musicians, we felt intensely proud of her. Avan soothes hearts
with her kindness and inspires others with her perseverance.

My Family Says...

Baran's World

I'm Baran, and My World Is Full of Color, Sounds and Sweet Smells!

Hi! I'm Baran Ghasemipoor, I'm ten years old, and I love everything that has to do with color, scent, and beautiful sounds. When I sit at the piano and my fingers dance across the keys, I feel like I'm creating a whole new world. The sound of the piano is like the sound of rain, calm yet full of energy!

Baking cakes is one of my favorite things to do, especially when I surprise my parents with a cake I've made myself.

When I see their smiling faces, I feel the most wonderful joy in the world. I also love finger knitting and crafting, always trying to make things that are both beautiful and useful. Even when I play games, I'm always looking for smarter and more creative ways to move through the levels one after another.

What Makes Me Special

One of the things that makes me special is my connection with animals. Every animal, even the ones that others might be afraid of, seems to calm down when I'm around. It feels like they can understand what's in my heart. I take care of them and dream that one day I'll be able to help all animals everywhere.

I also love reading books. Sometimes I read for hours, completely lost in the world of stories without ever feeling tired. Books are like windows that open into new worlds for me. If I had a whole day to myself, I'd love to spend it with my friends, starting with burgers at a restaurant, followed by a trip to the cinema and an amusement park, and finishing off with lots of snacks and some shopping! I really love trying new experiences!

Kindness and Teamwork at School

To me, being a good friend means protecting your friends, being kind to them,
and staying by their side when they're sad. Sometimes I write letters to my friends
and draw little pictures with them to make them happy.
At home, I always try to help my parents. For instance, once my mom
and I vacuumed the house together, and baked a cake.
The sweet smell filled the house, and everything felt brighter and happier.

At school, if I see trash on the ground, I pick it up. I even have a small flowerpot
that I once took to school and placed in the classroom to make the space more beautiful.
My teachers say I'm always looking for ways to make my surroundings
a nicer and more cheerful place.

My Big Dreams

I love animals, and when I grow up,
I want to become a veterinarian.
I want to help animals that are sick
or have lost a leg so they can live more
comfortably. Maybe I'll even become
a doctor one day and help people
recover from diseases. I genuinely
believe that everyone can help make
the world a safer place; all it takes is
a sincere desire to do good.
If I could give one piece of advice
to people everywhere, I would say:
"Keep the Earth clean and take care
of nature and animals, because they
need kindness just as much as we do."
If I were a superhero, I'd love to have
the power to fly, and my dog would
be able to fly too! Together, we'd travel
all around the world. With my magical
powers, I'd give strength to those
in need, fight against evil, and make
the world a safer place. On this adventure,
my sister Avan would always be by my side.
We'd visit Italy, France, and all the beautiful
places in the world, helping people and
animals wherever we go. Avan is one of the
most important people in my life!

I'm Baran, and I create my own world with
music, color, kindness, and imagination;
calm like the rain, and strong like the winds.

Baran is a girl with an always active and curious mind.
Whenever she faces a problem, she approaches it calmly and thoughtfully,
and she always finds a way to solve it. Her analytical skills and concentration
are remarkable, and she learns new things with incredible speed.
From her very first piano lessons, she practiced with enthusiasm and
dedication, and now the sound of her playing fills our home like
a gentle breeze. For Baran, swimming and basketball are not just hobbies;
they are ways to become stronger and to challenge herself.
This determination and drive to improve can be seen in everything
she does. One of the moments we were most proud of her was when
her team project was selected among the top entries at the
Scratch Global Competition in England. Through that experience,
she tested her creativity and perseverance on an international level.
Baran has a kind heart. Once, when her friend had a broken leg,
she didn't wait to be asked for help; she patiently and gently
helped her up and down the stairs. Baran always tries to share what
she knows with others, especially with younger children.
And there's a funny little thing about her: some nights, when she's
supposed to be asleep, she secretly turns on a small light under
her blanket and reads a book. Maybe it's in those quiet moments
that her imagination begins to bloom, the same imagination that
makes her such a curious, bright, and wonderfully creative girl.

My Family Says...

Mersana's World

I am Mersana, and I Love Singing and Dancing

Hi! My name is Mersana Hajhosseini, and I'm nine years old. I love to move, learn, and help.

I enjoy dancing, singing, and talking with people, and I am so active that I often walk more than 10,000 steps per day. My friends and teachers say I am great at reading, doing math, solving problems, helping everybody, and even finding things that go missing. I feel happiest when I am running, when I finish my homework on time, when I visit my family, and when I treat myself to something like an ice cream after a good day.

What I'm Proud of

I am friendly, kind, and thoughtful. I try to show that every day by the way I listen, help, and use my brain to figure things out. If I could teach someone something I know well, I would teach math and dancing. Math makes me feel calm and clever, and dancing makes me feel free and strong. Some skills were challenging at first, such as fractions, times tables, and swimming. I kept practicing until they finally made sense, and now I feel proud when I solve a tricky problem or swim across the pool.

Things I Love

I love spending time outdoors and with friends. I could spend all day at Wonderland or Disneyland with them, swimming at the pool, camping in nature, or going on road trips. I also enjoy playing on my iPad to relax.

Another thing I would love is to have a puppy, because I adore animals and would enjoy playing with and taking care of one.

How I Care and Help

To me, being a good friend means you can be trusted. You are kind. You do not lie or fight. I try to bring peace rather than arguments. Once, I helped someone who was about to fall, and nothing bad happened because I caught her in time. That made me feel helpful and proud.

I want the world to have less fighting and more peace, so I try to be a kind person everywhere I go. In the future, I hope to be strong enough to stand up to bad people and not let them hurt others.

If I could help one person, it would be my mom. If she got sick, I would pay her bills and, if she needed it, I would be the surgeon who helped her get better.

Dreaming Big

When I grow up, I want to have a big, warm heart
that helps others, and I aspire to be a brain surgeon who saves lives.
I also want to be a good mom to my five kids and have enough money
to help children who don't have parents, so they can feel safe and loved.
I want to be a professor too, so I can teach others to be helpful and kind
and to use their knowledge for good. I dream of living on a big farm
with many animals that I care for every day.
The difference I hope to make is to continue learning and
staying active, and to utilize those skills to benefit people
and the environment.

If I could teach the whole world one lesson, it would be simple:
no smoking, no drinking, and please keep the world and the sky clean.
Sometimes I imagine a superhero version of me.
My powers would be strength, speed, and invisibility, and I would also be
able to control fire and nature. With those powers, I would save the world
from bad people and protect anyone who needs help. I would not do it alone.
I would bring two of my closest friends with me so we could work
as a team and watch out for each other.

I am Mersana, and every day,
I try to use my heart, my mind, and
my energy to make life brighter for
the people and animals around me.

Mersana is a child full of energy, curiosity, and heart.
She is naturally talented at dancing and loves to try new things whenever the opportunity arises. She is very smart, kind, honest, respectful, and dependable, and she has a gift for expressing her thoughts clearly and connecting with people around her.
One of her greatest strengths is her ability to quickly see solutions where others might only notice difficulties, demonstrating maturity well beyond her years.
One of the most memorable moments of her kindness was when her cousin came to Canada from Iran three years ago.
At that time, her cousin was unable to speak English. Although speaking Farsi was difficult for Mersana, she immediately switched to Farsi during the entire visit to make her cousin feel more comfortable. As soon as her cousin left, she naturally went back to English again.

My Family Says...

Watching her make that sacrifice to ease someone else's
feelings was a powerful reminder of her empathy.
We've been proud to see her conquer her fear of swimming.
At first, she was scared of going into the pool, but with
determination, she learned to enjoy it with confidence.
She also amazes us with her ability to love herself.
It's inspiring to see how confident she is becoming.
At home, Mersana's cheerful, talkative nature fills our days,
and we truly miss her when she's away.
She deeply cares for her brother and always looks after him.
At school, her kindness wins her many friends.
A unique quality about her is her maturity;
even at such a young age, she carries herself with wisdom
and thoughtfulness that surprise us every day.

My Family Says...

Deniz's World

I'm Deniz, in Love with the Ocean and with Life!

Hi! My name is Deniz Hajirasouli, and I'm nine years old.
For as long as I can remember, the sea has been a world full of peace
and mystery for me. I love swimming, gymnastics, and painting, and
whenever I'm in the water, I feel free and strong, just like a fish at home!
Every time I learn a new move and dive into the water,
I feel a special kind of joy.
Reading, especially about nature and the oceans, is something I never
get tired of. I love learning new things. Right now, I'm improving my English
and French, and whenever I pronounce a complex sentence correctly,
I feel like I've taken a big step forward.

One morning, something incredible happened, a snowy white owl flew by my window and dropped a letter with a golden seal. It said I had been accepted to Hogwarts School of Witchcraft and Wizardry! I could hardly believe my eyes. A few weeks later, with my suitcase packed and my cat Adrina curled up beside me, I boarded the Hogwarts Express. As the train began to move, I watched the world rush by and felt like I was traveling between reality and a dream, between the ordinary and the magical.

Painting and Adventure

For me, painting is like a colorful adventure. Every time I pick up my brush, a story begins to take shape in my mind. Sometimes I paint people and animals, and sometimes the ocean and the little fish hiding among the corals and sometimes Hogwarts School. Once, my art teacher told me that the doll I had made was lovely. In that moment, I felt that I could truly create things that make others happy.

My friends and teachers often describe me as someone who works with great care and persistence. I also have a strong passion for math because I enjoy the challenge of solving problems. Each one feels like a puzzle whose pieces I can assemble through careful thinking, and finding the correct answer gives me a deep sense of excitement and satisfaction. Math has taught me patience, focus, and the joy of discovery.

Kindness and Courage

I believe that one of the most essential things in life is to be kind and
to help others. Once, my sister fell into the water, and I was able to save her.
In that moment, I realized that a person must always stay calm and brave
to help others. There have also been times when I've helped my
classmates' teams during sports competitions to ensure their success.
For me, working together and supporting others matters more than any victory.
I always try to keep my friends' secrets and listen carefully when they talk,
because to me, a good friend is someone who can be trusted.
Sometimes, just being by your friends side is enough
to make them feel stronger! I also dream of helping all the children
who don't have families and finding loving homes for them.

Love for Nature and Animals

One of the most essential things in my life is nature, from the trees and the sea to my cat, Adrina, who is like a true friend to me. Adrina always calms me with her eyes. I believe that animals have feelings too, and that we must take care of them. If I could give one piece of advice to people around the world, it would be that no one has the right to harm nature or animals. I have an idea in mind: one day, I want to create a special channel about the Pacific Ocean and explain to everyone how we can protect the sea and its ice. I wish the world would change so that there would be no waste left on land or in the water, and all living beings could live together in peace.

My Big Dreams

When I think about the future, a thousand beautiful pictures come to my mind!
I want to be a diver, an astronaut, a traveler, and an actor! I dream of exploring
the world, from the depths of the ocean to the vastness of space. I want to help
nature breathe again and keep the seas clean.

I aspire to be a calm person inside, yet when necessary, I want to be as powerful
and unpredictable as the ocean. I hope always to be thoughtful, caring, and kind.
If I were a superhero, I would want to breathe both in space and under the sea,
talk to cats, have supernatural powers, and bring peace and life wherever I go.
I would love to travel with Adrina and my friends, visit oceans and planets,
and take care of the earth and the sky. I'm only nine years old, but every day
I'm learning how to move like a wave, strong, calm, and beautiful, and to
make the world a better place.

I'm Deniz, a dreamer who finds
peace in the sea and hope in
every wave. I believe that even
the gentlest ripple
can bring light and
change to the world.

Deniz is a kind and gentle girl who always pays attention to others.
When someone is sad, she feels it too and tries to talk to them or hug them
to make them feel better. She is especially patient with her little sister
and always looks after her. At home, Deniz makes everything brighter
with her kindness, whether she's sitting next to her cat, Adrina,
or carefully watering the flowers so they don't wilt.
Deniz has a quick and creative mind. She enjoys solving math problems
and loves understanding the logic behind them. When she swims,
it's as if she becomes one with the water, calm, focused, and fearless.
Lately, she's been making significant progress in her acting and gymnastics
classes, learning each new move with her own extraordinary enthusiasm.
One funny thing about Deniz is that she believes she can talk to cats!
She also loves the Harry Potter books and movies and is waiting for
the day when her letter of acceptance to the School of Witchcraft
and Wizardry (Hogwarts) finally arrives!
We are always proud of Deniz, whether she's patiently caring for
animals or thoughtfully solving complex problems. Deniz has a
world of her own, a world full of kindness, imagination, and beauty.

My Family Says...

Amirhossein's World

I'm Amirhossein: I Love Soccer and Building New Things!

Hi! I'm Amirhossein Heidari, and I'm 10 years old. Ever since I was very little, a soccer ball has been one of my best friends. Whenever I play, I feel like the world belongs to me! I usually play as the goalkeeper for my team. I chose this position because I love the excitement of that split second when the ball is rushing toward the goal, and I have to decide, quickly and with full focus, what to do. When I catch the ball and hear my teammates cheering, it feels like a thousand stars light up inside me. For me, soccer isn't just a game; it's a way to practice patience, concentration, and teamwork.

Besides soccer, I really enjoy playing on the trampoline. When I jump up and down, I think I'm flying, and the world beneath me gets smaller and smaller. Sometimes my friends and I have contests to see who can jump the highest. I also love riding my bike in the yard or on the street, enjoying the speed. At first, biking was challenging for me, I fell a few times, but now I'm really good at it, and every time I pedal, it is incredible.

A Creative Mind and Skillful Hands

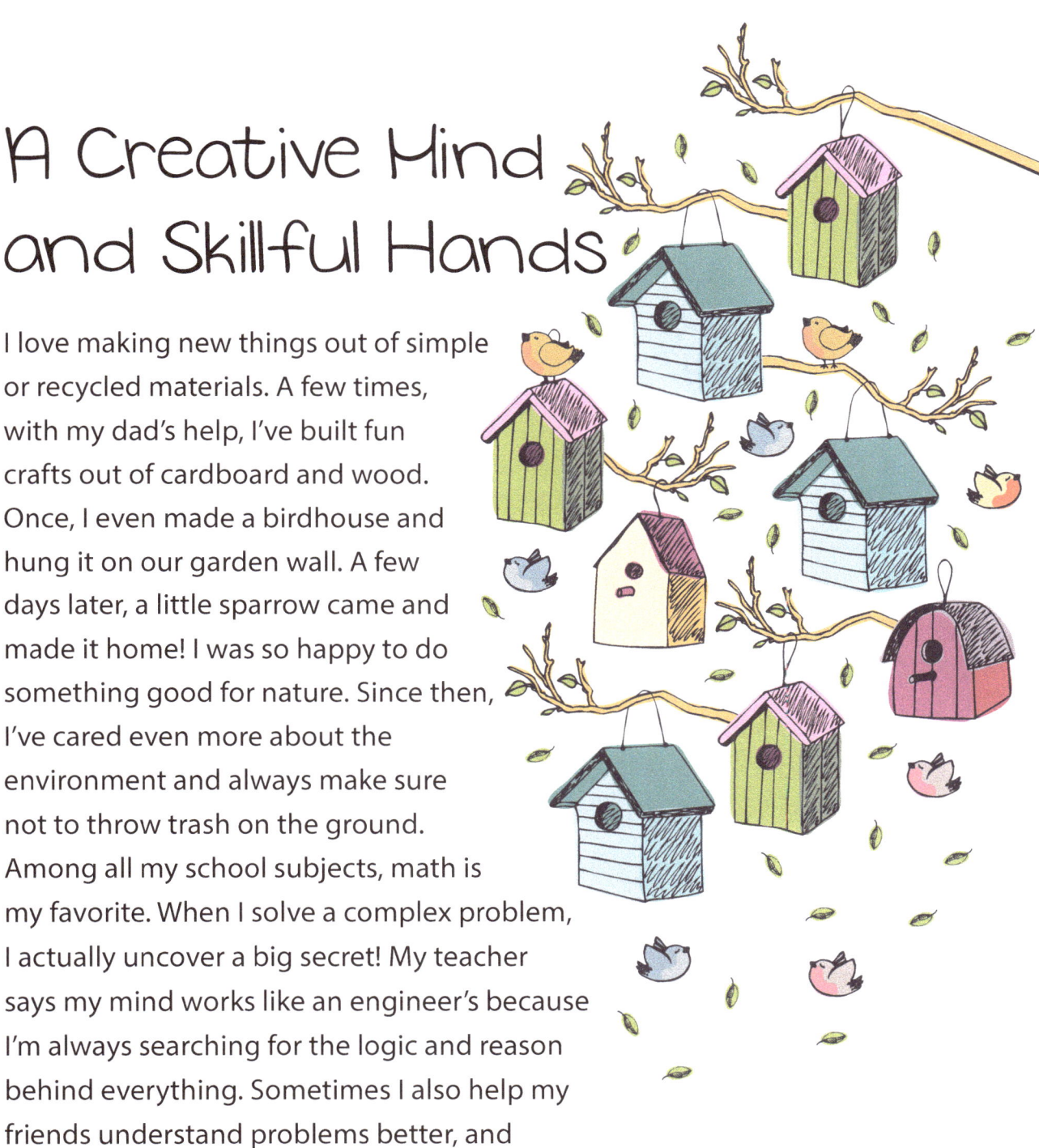

I love making new things out of simple or recycled materials. A few times, with my dad's help, I've built fun crafts out of cardboard and wood. Once, I even made a birdhouse and hung it on our garden wall. A few days later, a little sparrow came and made it home! I was so happy to do something good for nature. Since then, I've cared even more about the environment and always make sure not to throw trash on the ground. Among all my school subjects, math is my favorite. When I solve a complex problem, I actually uncover a big secret! My teacher says my mind works like an engineer's because I'm always searching for the logic and reason behind everything. Sometimes I also help my friends understand problems better, and we practice together.

Playing and Imagination

In my free time, if I'm not at an amusement park or a restaurant,
I'm usually playing PlayStation 4 or Minecraft.
For me, Minecraft isn't just a game; it's a vast world where I can build
anything I want: a house, a tower, a castle, or even a whole city! Every time
I design something new in the game, I feel one step closer to becoming
an engineer. This game helps me think more creatively, especially
when I have to use limited materials to build something big.

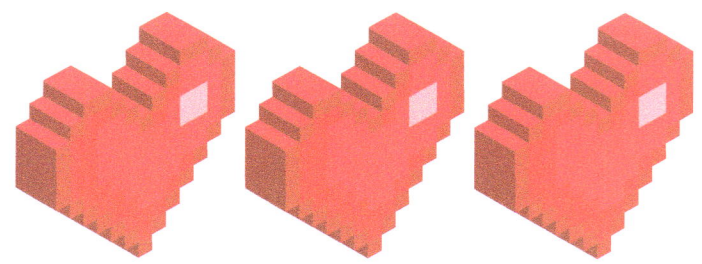

Kindness and Caring for Others

I can't stand seeing people upset. If my friend is sad, I hug him and
try to help him feel better. Once, one of my classmates got a bad grade
and felt really down. I shared my snacks with him and suggested that we
study together for the next test so he could get a better score.
I think that's what kindness really means: caring about how others feel.
I also love animals. Whenever I see a bird or a dog walking down the street,
I want to make sure they're okay and have something to eat.

My Big Dreams

When I grow up, I want to become an engineer and a football player. I want to build things that help people. Maybe one day I'll invent a machine that can turn waste into useful materials so nature won't be harmed as much. Alongside engineering, I'll keep playing soccer because it has taught me how to get back up and keep going after every defeat!

If I were a superhero, I'd love to have the power to fly. I'd be really strong and able to save people in dangerous situations. I'd form a team with Superman, Spider-Man, and Batman, and together we'd stand up to anyone who harms people or nature. If I could, I'd make sure no one ever felt sad and that the Earth always stayed clean and full of trees.

I'm still a kid, but I believe that anyone can make the world a better place with kindness, creativity, and determination. Maybe that's the real power of superheroes!

I'm Amirhossein, and maybe I don't wear a cape, but with my soccer ball, my tools, and my big heart, I think I already have a bit of superhero power!

Amirhossein is a boy whose kindness and deep understanding
of others' feelings always amaze us. He's kind to everyone,
his friends, people in need, and anyone else who might need help.
Whenever he sees someone struggling, he doesn't hesitate to lend
a hand. His empathy fills his world with friends and smiles,
and he's always the first to start a friendship.
Adaptability and patience are among Amirhossein's special traits.
He knows that achieving goals takes time and focus.
Once he makes a decision, he stays committed to it until the end.
This persistence shows in everything he does, from schoolwork to play
to building creative projects. He's also very organized in all his activities.
One moment that made us truly proud was when, after a difficult day,
he sincerely thanked us for our efforts. That's when we realized
how much he had grown. A funny thing about Amirhossein is that
he never gives up until he finishes what he's started!
He's determined and hardworking, just like a little hero.

My Family Says...

Amytis's World

I'm Amytis, and I Love My Culture!

Hi! My name is Amytis Heidari, and I'm eight years old. I love my Persian culture, and even my name is unique, which makes me feel special. Amytis is the name of a Persian princess; it also means a precious gem, and in Persian it carries the phrase "Holder of Good Thoughts," which reflects goodness of thought.

I'm the kind of person who wants to grow up to be very friendly, respectful, independent, and responsible. I care deeply about my family, my friends, and the world around me. Whether I'm studying math, playing volleyball, or braiding my own hair, I always try my best and keep learning new things every day.

I also speak Spanish, in addition to English, and can both speak and write it. Additionally, I am fluent in Persian and enjoy reading poetry in Farsi. For me, languages are a way to connect with more people and make more impact.

My Passions

One of the things that makes me happiest is volleyball. Whenever I'm on the court, I feel full of energy and confidence. I could play all day without getting bored! Math is another area I'm really good at, and I feel proud when I solve problems quickly. I also love talking about movies and shows I've seen, because stories inspire me and give me ideas about life. And one thing I worked really hard at was braiding my own hair, now I'm fantastic at it, and it shows me that practice really does pay off.

Caring for the World

I care a lot about saving the environment and try to work harder to protect it every day. At school and at home, I remind myself to respect nature and to use less waste, because I want the earth to stay clean and safe. I believe even small actions, like picking up trash or recycling, can make a big difference if we all do them. More than anything, I want to help my family. If they ever feel like giving up, I want to be the one to keep them positive and encourage them to stay strong

My Big Dreams

When I think about my future, I want to become an engineer like my mom and dad. I hope to use what I learn to make the world a better place to live. I also dream of being someone who lifts others, helping people rise when they are feeling down. That's the kind of difference I want to make in the future.

If I could be a superhero, my power would be mind control, because it includes everything, helping, protecting, and making positive changes. As a superhero, I would stop violence and save the world from harm. I imagine traveling anywhere I'm needed, making peace, and spreading kindness. I wouldn't need a big team, just my determination to protect people, nature, and the future.

I'm Amytis, and I might not wear a crown like the Persian princess I'm named after, but I shine my own way, through kindness, courage, and love!

Amytis is a mature, responsible, and kind child. She has a caring heart, strong faith, and a deep sense of gratitude that shines through in everything she does. Even at a young age, her maturity shows in how she expresses herself, makes decisions, and connects with others. One of the moments that touches us most is how she looks after us when we are unwell. She does her best to care, demonstrating her natural thoughtfulness and love.

Recently, we've seen her grow in gratitude and her commitment to daily prayer, which makes us proud of the person she is becoming. In fact, the proudest moment for us is simply introducing her as our daughter, because she represents so many excellent qualities. Another source of pride is when she practices and reads sophisticated Persian poems in front of family and friends. Everyone admires her confidence, which showcases her deep love and appreciation for her Persian culture. At home and at school, she makes a difference with her maturity, kindness, and responsibility. And, of course, she has a fun and creative side; she can spend hours seriously studying and at the same time, hours building with Legos, always inventing something new.

My Family Says...

Diba's
World

I'm Diba, in Love with Learning and New Experiences!

Hi! My name is Diba Hosseiniasl, I'm 12 years old, and I love discovering, experimenting, and creating new things! For me, every day is like a blank page waiting to be filled with new colors. When I play the violin, I feel as if I'm speaking through the notes, painting a world of emotions.

The first time I performed in a concert hall in front of a hundred people, my heart was racing, but when I saw the audience smiling, I realized that music lets me connect with people's hearts.

I speak Persian, English, and French, and I love talking with people from different countries; it gives me a sense of harmony with the world. I'm passionate about abacus math, programming, painting, and adventure. The abacus has taught me focus and discipline, while programming gives me a sense of creativity, as it allows me to build something out of nothing, and it can make life easier.

I also hold a green belt in self-defence martial arts. The belt itself doesn't matter much to me, but having the ability to defend myself feels empowering, and I'm proud of that.

Loyalty, Honesty and Helping Others

I believe loyalty and honesty are among my most important qualities.
When I make a promise to someone, I do everything I can to keep it.
To me, being honest means taking responsibility for my actions, even when
I've made a mistake. Once, I didn't pass the exam for gifted students, but
instead of feeling upset, I talked with my parents about what went wrong
and decided to practice more so I could succeed next time.
Helping others gives me a deep sense of joy and confidence.
For example, in class, when the teacher asks someone to explain a topic,
I often volunteer. And when a friend struggles with a lesson or a task,
I stay with them until they understand. I believe that supporting others
makes the world around me a better place. Once, someone was making
fun of my friend, and I stood up for them, telling the person, politely,
that this behavior wasn't right.
My teachers often tell me, "You have a bright future ahead of you, and we can't
wait for the day when we can proudly say you were our student!"

Everyday Life and Adventure

I love order and cleanliness. I like my room to be tidy, with every book and item in its place, and I enjoy having my day follow a plan. But alongside that sense of order, I also love adventure.

I dream of traveling the world with my parents, visiting museums and historical sites, and eating ice cream at the top of the Eiffel Tower when we reach Paris! I enjoy cooking, especially when I can make food that's both delicious and healthy. The sound of music at home, reading books, and learning new things all give me energy. For me, no day should ever be exactly like the one before; each day should bring something to learn, something to grow from, and something new to discover and talk about!

Making the World More Beautiful

If we want to make a difference
in this world, we have to help make it a
more beautiful place. At home, I help with
chores, and at school, I treat everyone with
respect and encourage my friends not to
give up when things get difficult.
I'm also kind to animals. When I'm outside,
I feed hungry pigeons, cats, or dogs.
I believe kindness is like a chain that begins
with a single smile and reaches all the way
to the farthest corners of the world.

My Big Dreams

I have big dreams. I want to become a neurosurgeon so I can help
patients regain their health. At the same time, I love writing because it allows me
to share my feelings with others through words. My greatest dream is to one day become
a peace ambassador, so that people around the world can live together
without war or borders. I want to help create a world that is not only
more beautiful but also kinder, built with knowledge, creativity, and compassion.
If I could create a superhero version of myself, Super Diba would have a solution
for every war and every illness. I would be able to read people's minds to
understand their pain and heal them, and I could fly so that I'd be present
everywhere in the world, helping both humans and animals. On every journey,
my parents would be by my side, because without them,
none of my dreams would feel complete.

I am Diba, a girl who wants to build a
world filled with both peace and knowledge,
guided by honesty, discipline, curiosity,
and love for the world.

From early childhood, Diba has had a calm spirit and a bright heart. Her kindness doesn't come from fleeting emotions but from a deep understanding of what it means to be human. She has strong emotional intelligence and can recognize and manage both her own feelings and those of others in different situations. This ability allows her to connect easily with people and make new friends wherever she goes. At the same time, her peaceful nature is so strong that, even as a child, she sometimes had to learn that forgiveness isn't always the only correct answer.

One of our sweetest memories of her is from the day she was playing with her cousin. When she noticed he was upset after losing several times in a row, she deliberately lost the next round just to see happiness return to his eyes. That small but profound gesture captures Diba's essence, compassionate, empathetic, and deeply humane. Diba has a passionate and inquisitive mind. She pursues her interests in artificial intelligence, music, and foreign languages with focus and determination. From the age of six, when she won second place in an international abacus competition, to the day she advanced beyond her grade level, she has consistently shown that growth and learning are at the heart of who she is. For Diba, cleanliness, order, and respect for the environment aren't duties, they are a way of life. Even now, she still lines up her dolls and teaches them lessons, just as she did when she was little. Perhaps in that endless game lies the quiet beginning of her future as a teacher, a writer, and a leader.

My Family Says...

Selena's World

I'm Selena, and I'm Kind!

Hi! I'm Selena Hosseinzadeh, and I'm eight years old.

I love animals, nature, and spending time with my family and friends.

I try to be kind and caring, and I like making new friends. Dancing,
gymnastics, and singing make me feel full of energy.

I also like solving math problems and keeping things tidy.

Most of all, I love being myself and spreading kindness wherever I go.

What Makes Me Shine

I'm really proud of my skills in dancing, singing, and gymnastics.
They make me feel both strong and creative. In gymnastics, it took
a lot of work to learn new moves, but I kept trying, and now I can do things
like cartwheels and other challenging moves. Math used to be challenging
for me, but I practiced until I got really good at it, and now I enjoy teaching
multiplication to others. I'm also proud of being organized,
I love putting things in order and keeping everything neat.
My teachers say I'm great at making friends,
which makes me feel truly special.

What I Love

I love going on trips with my family, especially when we go to resorts with water parks or to the beach. Swimming and playing in the water make me so happy! I also love to read and could spend hours with my favorite books. And I can talk forever about the musical I'm acting in, it's about K-pop demon hunters, and I'm so excited about it!

My Kind Heart

What makes me special is that I'm compassionate and fair to others.
I believe being a good friend means sharing, caring, and ensuring others
feel happy, and that's what I try to do every day. I once helped a friend who
fell and got hurt by taking her to the office and making sure she was safe.
I also take care of myself by doing things that make me feel good,
like playing with my friends and family.

At home, I help with chores and dishes, and at school, I work hard,
respect others, and try to set a good example. For the world, I want to protect
animals and nature, and make sure our Earth remains clean and beautiful.

My Big Dreams

When I grow up, I want to be an actress and a voice actor. I want to use my voice to tell stories and bring happiness and hope to others. I also dream of inspiring others to be considerate, brave, and caring. If I could teach the world one lesson, it would be to respect nature, love animals, and always stand up for what's right. If I could, I'd support those with unfair leaders, empowering them to seek peace and protect their rights. If I were a superhero, I'd have the power of teleportation so I could go anywhere in the world in an instant. I'd travel to places where people and animals need help, and I'd make sure nature is protected. I'd bring my family and friends with me so we could all work together to make the world a better place.

I am Selena, and I believe that with kindness, courage, and a caring heart, we can all make a difference.

Selena is full of energy, courage, and heart. From an early age, she has shown a natural talent for physical activities, excelling in swimming, gymnastics, and dance. She has an adventurous spirit and is never afraid to take risks, whether she's trying a new move in gymnastics or tackling a new challenge at school. Her independence shines through in the way she approaches life; she's confident, capable, and determined to give her very best in everything she does.

What makes Selena truly special, though, is her generous and compassionate heart. She deeply cares about others and always wants to help. We have seen this in the way she supports her friends, especially those who are shy or struggling, encouraging them to be brave and reminding them that they are not alone. She also loves to give back, whether it's putting effort into a charity project at school or helping with fundraisers. Her generosity and thoughtfulness have a profound impact on everyone around her.

We take pride in Selena every single day, not only for her talents and achievements, but also for the person she is becoming. Her courage to connect with others, her empathy, and her positivity inspire us. At home, she brings joy and laughter, always eager to help and always ready with a joke that makes us laugh out loud. At school and in the community, she makes a difference by spreading joy and confidence wherever she goes. Selena is growing into a compassionate, strong, and confident young girl, and we couldn't be prouder of her.

My Family Says...

Sophia's World

I'm Sophia, and, I'm Unstoppable!

Hi! I'm Sophia Hosseinzadeh, and I'm 10 years old. I love nature, family, art, and meeting new people. Reading and writing are two of my favorite things; I can spend hours lost in a book or crafting stories of my own. I'm also someone who loves to perform, singing, acting, or even directing my own musical! Making friends comes easily to me, and I care deeply about helping people feel happy and included.

My Passions

I'm proud of how much I've grown as a writer and reader, they both give me confidence and joy. I feel happiest when I reread my own stories or listen to recordings of myself singing. My teachers and friends often say I'm great at creative writing, and I think they're right, it's something that comes naturally to me. Songwriting was hard at first, but now I feel really confident doing it. Acting is another passion of mine. I love performing and even teaching others how to act; right now, I'm directing and performing in a musical about K-pop demon hunters!

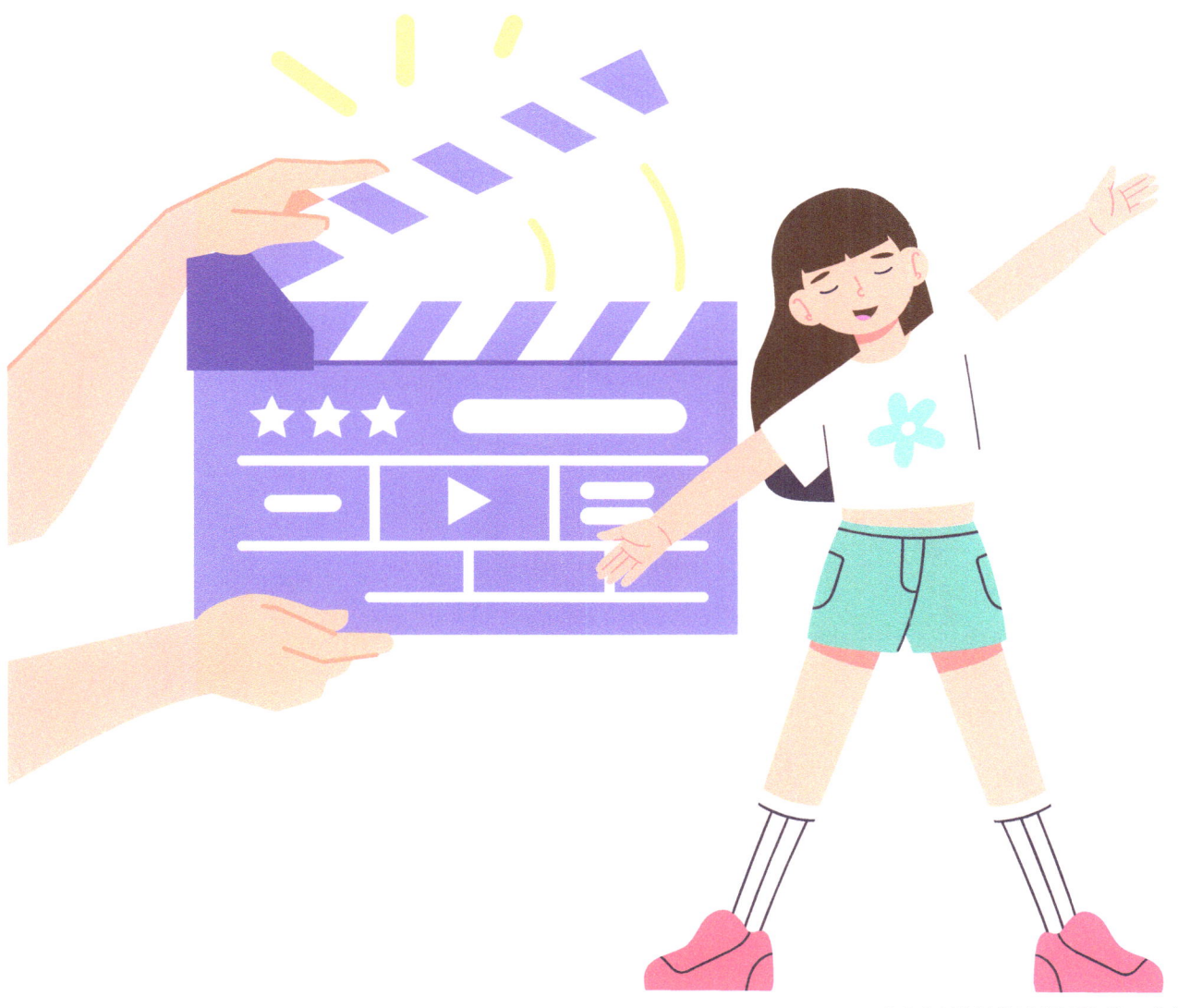

My Kind Side

One thing that makes me unique is my ability to connect with people easily.
I say hi, and soon we're spending time together. I think being a good friend
means truly caring, so I always try to listen and make my friends happy.
Once, when a friend was getting scared during a story I was telling,
I changed the ending so she wouldn't feel embarrassed or uncomfortable.
That moment reminded me how important it is to be thoughtful.

Caring about the World

I care deeply about nature and want to help keep the world clean and safe
for people and animals. If I could help someone right now,
I would adopt a dog without a home, feed it, and take it for walks
so it feels loved. Fairness matters to me because everyone deserves respect
and kindness. At home, at school, or anywhere I go, I try to follow the rules,
bring positivity, and do little things that make people smile.

My Big Dreams

When I grow up, I'd like to be an author, singer, or actor,
maybe even all three! I also dream of creating a sport just for girls, one that's
fun and challenging. If I could teach the world one lesson, it would be that
girls can play soccer and deserve to be passed the ball.
If I were a superhero, my power would be omnipotence. I'd use it to support
people and nations like North Koreans to live freely, with new laws
that allow them to travel, eat well, and enjoy their lives. I'd ask one kind
and caring person from every country to join me so we could share ideas,
stories, and ways to make life better. Together, we could make sure
no place in the world feels like a prison, and every person has the chance
to live with hope and happiness.

I am Sophia, and I believe that with
a kind heart and courage, we can bring
positive change wherever we are.

Sophia is a child full of creativity, determination, and heart.
From an early age, her writing talent has been remarkable. She expresses herself through words in a way that feels both unique and powerful. Beyond her writing, she is naturally bright and focused. Once she decides to achieve something, whether in academics, the arts, or sports, she works with persistence until she reaches her goal. Sophia also has strong leadership skills. At school, she takes the lead, creating clubs and bringing people together. She is detail-oriented and often helps us make decisions by comparing options and reviews. Over the past years, we've seen Sophia grow in ways that make us deeply proud. She has become more aware of her emotions and learned to embrace them as part of who she is. Instead of trying to be perfect, she now focuses on doing her best and appreciating herself along the way.

Sophia's caring side shines in her relationships, especially with her sister. One touching moment was when her sister lost her hat in a store and wasn't allowed to get a treat. Sophia used her own money to buy the Sour Patch candies her sister wanted to make her smile. We'll never forget how she shone on stage during her first performance. She carried herself with confidence and passion, demonstrating the significant growth she had achieved. Her thoughtfulness also extends to our community. It was Sophia's idea to build a little free library in front of our house so neighbors could share the books she treasures. Of course, Sophia also has a wonderful sense of humor. Mimicking my voice and mannerisms always makes us laugh. Whether she is writing, leading, caring for her sister, or making us laugh, Sophia continues to amaze us with her creativity, compassion, and ability to inspire others.

My Family Says...

Aynaz's World

I'm Aynaz, and I'm Creative

Hi, I'm Aynaz Hozourbakhsh, and I'm 12 years old. I've always felt proud of my
artistic skills, whether it's drawing, writing poetry, or playing the piano.
One of my proudest accomplishments was being selected for the Talent for
Writing program, where my poem was published in Wonder Words: US Poets.
My friends and teachers often say I'm talented in writing and art,
which encourages me to keep going.
I feel the happiest and most confident when I play piano in front of
my family and friends. Sharing music with them fills me with joy and makes me
feel a sense of connection. Something I could easily teach others is character design,
because I love creating unique personalities and stories. Tennis is also
a significant part of my life, although it was challenging at first. I've worked hard,
and now I'm proud of how good I've become. If you asked me what
makes me special, I'd say it's my ability to come up with strong and creative ideas.

Kindness from the Heart

If I had a whole day to myself, I'd spend it with my family and relatives, because being with them always makes me happy, and their encouragement and guidance keep me moving toward my goals.
I also love spending time with friends. To me, being a good friend means standing by them through every challenge. I support my friends by being kind, listening, and helping in any way I can. Once, when a classmate had to leave during a lesson, I wrote all the notes for her so she wouldn't miss anything. Small acts of kindness like that remind me how even little things can make a big difference.
Kindness is something I value a lot. I care deeply about protecting people's feelings and making sure I don't hurt anyone with my words or actions. Being thoughtful is part of who I am.

Caring about the World

The world around us is something I often think about.
I want to help keep Earth clean and healthy, because everyone
deserves a safe environment. I also care about fairness and
about helping those who don't have enough.
If I could, I would help people in poor communities
by providing them with food, clean water, safe housing,
good schools, and also space for joy and entertainment.
At home and at school, I try to spread positivity.
I believe staying kind and supportive makes
our community stronger. Even small actions, such as
encouraging others or maintaining a good attitude,
can create a wave of happiness.

If I had a superhero version of myself, my extraordinary power
would be the ability to communicate with animals.
I imagine using that gift to build stronger connections between
humans and nature. As a superhero, I would travel to places suffering
from war and famine, bringing hope and practical support. I would take
my mother and father with me, because they are my source of strength.

My Big Dreams

When I grow up, I would like to become an eye doctor, but I also want to continue creating art on the side. Art has the power to bring people together, and I want to share its beauty with others. I also dream of helping build a future with less war and less pollution, because both peace and the environment are essential to me. If I could teach the world one lesson, it would be to live with less stress and more joy, focusing on the little moments that bring happines.

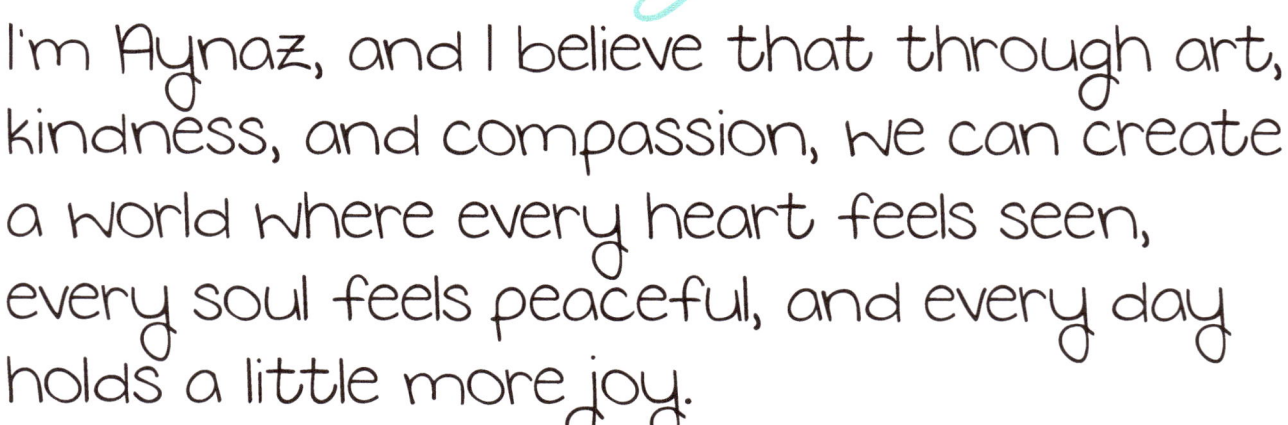

I'm Aynaz, and I believe that through art, kindness, and compassion, we can create a world where every heart feels seen, every soul feels peaceful, and every day holds a little more joy.

Aynaz is a child full of creativity, determination, and heart.
From a young age, she has demonstrated a natural talent for drawing
and generating unique and original ideas. What makes her stand out most
is her hardworking and intelligent nature. Once she commits to something,
she rarely gives up, no matter how difficult it might be.
Her persistence and focus make her a child who can take on challenges
with courage and see them through to the end.
One act of kindness we will never forget happened before an
international trip. With so many preparations to make, I was
overwhelmed, but Aynaz stepped in to help without being asked.
She took responsibility for packing, organizing, and even preparing meals
for her father, who couldn't travel with us. Her thoughtfulness and
maturity transformed a stressful time into something manageable,
and it revealed how deeply she cares about her family.
Recently, we've seen her grow through her dedication to piano lessons,
her enthusiasm for tennis, and her commitment to regular
exercise and biking. She impresses us with her ability to manage
her time carefully, balancing school, music, sports, and family life.
Some of our proudest moments come when she plays the piano
in public, carrying herself with confidence and grace, or when others
praise her for being wise, thoughtful, and kind. At home,
she makes a difference by bringing joy, lending a helping hand when
needed, and surprising us with handmade gifts and creative
games that showcase just how much love and imagination
she carries in her heart.

My Family Says...

Ava's World

I'm Ava, and I'm Bold and Brave!

Hi! My name is Ava Khalifeh, and I'm eight years old.
I have so many passions and dreams for the future.
I'm really good at presenting my projects at school and giving speeches in front of people. Standing up and sharing my ideas makes me feel proud and confident.
Speaking in front of a group isn't always easy, but I enjoy the challenge, and each time I do it, I feel even stronger.

My Passions

Art is one of my biggest passions. I enjoy drawing, painting, designing, and listening to music while working on my art. I'm proud to teach others how to draw. Helping friends learn new techniques or showing them how to make something beautiful with just a pencil and some paper is exciting for me. My friends and teachers often tell me I'm really good at presenting ideas and expressing myself creatively.

When I'm not drawing, I love riding my bike around the neighborhood, reading books, watching TV or playing games with my family. Board games are one of my favorite ways to spend time together, because they always bring laughter and fun. I can also spend hours building with Legos, as I come up with a new idea every time I create something. And of course, I love shopping for candy or making special smoothies, little treats that always make me smile.

Caring and Curious

I care a lot about nature and animals. Being outdoors brings me
peace and happiness, and I'm committed to protecting the environment
so that animals and people can thrive in a safe, clean world.
I believe kindness is one of the most essential qualities a person can have.
To me, a good friend is someone who listens, shares, and helps you when you need it.
I try to be that kind of friend every day. I once helped my friend find her
lost pencil case, and it felt great knowing I had made her day easier.

One of the things I enjoy most is asking questions and being curious.
I enjoy learning how things work, understanding why they happen,
and exploring ways to learn more. My curiosity keeps me open to new ideas,
and I think it's one of the reasons I love books and projects so much.

My Big Dreams

When I think about the future, I imagine myself as a fashion designer, an artist, and a singer. Fashion design excites me because I love colors, patterns, and styles, and I want to create clothes that help people feel happy and confident. At the same time, I want to continue creating art, including painting, drawing, and designing, that brings joy and inspiration to others. But my dreams aren't just about jobs. I want to grow up to be someone who is open-minded and willing to take risks. I believe that being open-minded means listening to others, respecting different opinions, and always being ready to learn something new.

Being a risk-taker means having the courage to try, even when something feels hard or scary. Those are the qualities I want to carry with me as I grow older, because I think they will help me achieve my dreams and also help me become a kind, caring person. I also hope that through my work, I can earn money to help the poor and support charities, because making a difference in people's lives is just as important to me as following my passions.

My Super Self

If I were a superhero, I would love to soar through the sky and see everything from above. I would carry a magic wand that could make extraordinary things happen, and I would use my hands as a special power to protect people and help them when they need it most. My goal would always be to save the day and make the world a happier place.

I imagine myself in a beautiful castle where magical adventures happen. I wouldn't go alone, though, I would bring my puppy sidekick with me. Together, we would explore, help others, and make sure everyone feels safe.

I'm Ava, and I know I'm still young, but with my curiosity, courage, and big dreams, I'm ready to make the world brighter.

Ava is a caring, passionate, and supportive child who brings warmth and creativity into everything she does. From a young age, she has shown a special interest in art, often filling our home with drawings, designs, and imaginative creations. Her ability to dream big and pursue her passions makes us believe she will one day achieve incredible things.

One moment that stays with us is how naturally she steps in when her younger brother is upset. When we cannot calm him down, Ava often finds a way, whether by playing with him, distracting him, or simply showing him love. Her patience and empathy shine in those moments. Recently, we've also seen her grow into a respectful and well-mannered listener, someone who takes time to understand others and treats everyone with kindness.

We felt incredibly proud when Ava stood in front of more than a hundred people and confidently delivered a speech about the power of hard work in achieving family success. Her courage and presence inspired not only us but everyone in the room. At home and in our community, she makes a difference every day, especially in her brother's life. And of course, one of the sweetest things about her is how she loves styling her clothes and hair in unique, creative ways that always make us smile..

My Family Says...

Arghavan's World

I'm Arghavan, and I See the World in Colors and Flowers!

Hi! My name is Arghavan Khalili, and I'm nine years old. Maybe because my name is the name of a flower, I love flowers and colors too! I'm very good at calligraphy, and even though this is my first year studying in Canada and learning English, I can already do my math homework by myself, and that makes me proud.
I love swimming, gymnastics, and cycling. Sometimes I swim without a life jacket in the deeper parts, and whenever I learn a new move, I feel so happy.
Of course, I always do it under my coach's supervision and with complete care.
Playing the piano is also something I really enjoy; whenever my fingers touch the keys and the sound fills our home, I feel thrilled. I also love reading and cooking. Every time I make something delicious and see my family smiling, I feel pleased.

Kindness and Helping Others

I believe a good friend is someone who is honest, keeps their promises,
and stays by others when they need support. My teachers say that
I understand people's feelings and can help them. Once, I explained to my friend
how to do her math exercise, and I saw how happy she became.
When someone is new to school or doesn't know the language well, I like
to stay close to them and help so they don't feel alone. I always try to
be grateful and empathetic toward others.
Nature and animals are also very important to me. I do my best to
take care of nature so that it stays beautiful and healthy.

Designing My Room and Imagination

I love designing and decorating my room, arranging my books, choosing the colors of the cushions, and hanging my favorite pictures and frames on the walls. Whenever I organize something or give a new look to my things, I feel like a little designer. Decorating my room is also a form of creative expression for me. I believe these moments of imagination will help me be productive and successful in the future. Imagination is what makes humans different from all other living beings and expands the boundaries of our growth to infinity

My Big Dreams

I love book cafés. When I grow up, I want to have my own book café where I can sell books, meet new people, and create a space for others to talk and find peace.

Thinking about such a place makes me happy; it's a mix of books, tea, and kind people, and what could be more beautiful than that?

When I grow up, I also want to be a strong person who can help rebuild cities destroyed by war or disaster. I want to do something that makes the world a safer place. Whenever I see children living in war or insecurity, my heart aches for them, and I promise myself that one day I'll do everything I can to bring peace and calm to the world.

If I were a superhero, I would love to be able to fly and have a mask that gives me the courage to speak up for others and stand up for those who are weak. On these adventures, I would be joined by the people I love.

I am Arghavan, a girl with beautiful handwriting, a sharp mind for math, skillful hands that play the piano, and a kind heart that wants to make the world calmer and more beautiful.

Arghavan is a patient, kind, and hardworking girl who, in every situation, shows her inner calm and deep understanding of life through her actions. She is very empathetic and can truly understand the feelings of those around her. This quality makes her a warm and comforting presence among her friends and classmates.

Arghavan's skill in solving math problems is remarkable, and she often helps classmates who find the lessons difficult. In her first school year in Canada, despite the challenges of learning a new language and being far from her old friends, she managed, through perseverance and dedication, to build close and genuine connections with her teachers and new classmates, earning her teacher's admiration by the end of the year. The sentence her teacher said, "I'm proud to have such a hardworking and strong student," was deeply meaningful to us. With her patience and calm nature, Arghavan brings warmth to our home and is both a good friend and a beloved student at school.

She has a creative mind and an eye for detail, approaching everything she does with care and a sense of responsibility. Arghavan's great love of learning and her constant desire to grow inspire those around her and show that a bright future awaits her.

My Family Says...

Mauna's World

I'm Mauna, Dancing Through Life with Kindness

Hi! I'm Mauna Majidpour, I'm 12 years old, and I would describe myself as creative, thoughtful, and full of energy. I love spending time with my family and friends, but I also enjoy the quiet moments when I can draw, dance, or play piano.
I think being kind and respectful makes a big difference in the world, and I always try to live by that

I'm proud of the things I've learned and practiced over time. I'm really good at drawing, swimming, writing, and playing piano.

My friends and teachers say I'm kind, a good problem solver, and fun to be around.

One thing that makes me special is that no one else is exactly like me, everyone is unique in their own way, with different DNA, bodies, and minds. That's something I love to remember: being different is what makes us special.

What Makes Me Unique

My Passions

Dance is one of my favorite things in the world. When I first started, I didn't know what I was doing, but I practiced and worked hard. Now I've even won an award, which makes me feel proud and excited.

I also love drawing and could spend hours sketching faces, hands, and landscapes. Sometimes, I imagine teaching others how to draw too.

I find happiness in the little things, being with my friends, playing fun games, or curling up with my favorite movies.

Together

I feel happiest and most confident when I'm doing something familiar,
but I also love trying new things with the people I care about.
Helping others is important to me, whether it's walking a friend to the nurse
when they're hurt or simply listening when someone needs to talk.
At school, I try to make a difference by picking up rubbish with my friends
during breaks to keep our space clean. I believe kindness and fairness
are powerful, and I try to practice them every day.

My Big Dreams

When I think about the future, I imagine many paths.
I dream of being an architect, a private chef, or even
a surgeon, jobs where I can use both my creativity
and my love of helping people.
I also want to make a real difference in the environment
by fighting pollution and global warming so the planet can be
healthier for animals, nature, and people.
I would also help people who don't have many
opportunities or options by creating foundations
or donating money to support their
personal growth.

If I could teach the world one lesson, it would be this:
if you don't have something kind to say, stay quiet, and don't let
hurtful words from others take away your confidence or self-worth.
If I could create a superhero version of myself, I would be able to fly and
read minds. I'd soar through the city to help people in need,
making sure everyone feels safe and cared for. And yes, I'd definitely
stop by a donut shop in between missions!
Most of all, I'd want to be a superhero who inspires kindness, respect, and hope.

I'm Mauna, and I believe that spreading kindness and using our talents can make each day better for ourselves and those around us.

Mauna is a child who amazes us with her many talents and the way
she combines creativity, determination, and kindness.
From a very young age, her fine motor skills stood out,
whether she was dancing with poise, sketching with precision,
or writing with an unusually rich vocabulary.
Her passion for ballet has grown year by year, and reaching the
milestone of moving up to pointe shoes was a moment
of pride for our whole family.
For anyone unfamiliar, pointe shoes are special ballet shoes that
allow a dancer to perform on the very tips of their toes,
something that requires years of training, strength, and discipline.
Being ready for pointe work is a significant achievement for
any dancer, and Mauna reached it with dedication and grace.
This year, she was also recognized for her commitment to ballet
with a medal at her studio's annual performance,
another moment that filled us with pride.

My Family Says...

Mauna's thoughtful and considerate nature shows up in countless ways. She never forgets her teachers' special days, making cards to show her appreciation, and once even baking a cake for her Grade Six teachers.
She leads with kindness, both at home and at school, where she naturally takes on a leadership role among her peers. She encourages her friends, supports her teachers, and quietly sets an example through her values and actions.
There is also a funny side to Mauna's independence. If she is hungry, she doesn't wait for anyone, she heads to the kitchen and cooks something herself. She's already a confident little chef! All these qualities, her creativity, kindness, leadership, independence, and commitment, make us proud every day. Mauna is growing into someone who not only has talent but also the heart and determination to make a difference.

My Family Says...

Pararin's World

I'm Pararin, and My Art Makes the World Smile!

Hi! My name is Pararin Modarresi Yazdi, I'm eight years old, and I love painting, making 3D crafts, playing instruments and cooking.
Painting makes me feel calm, I love colors, and every time I create a beautiful painting, I feel proud of myself. When I build a box or a small sculpture out of paper and cardboard, I feel like a little inventor! Whenever I pick up a brush or work with scissors and glue, I feel like I can do anything and create whatever I imagine.

Playing the piano was difficult for me at first, but now I really enjoy it and would love to teach it to others one day. Whenever I play the piano after all the years I have practiced, I feel like a storyteller telling a tale through music and the dance of fingers.

Making desserts also feels like a game to me, a spoon, a bowl, a bit of cream, and the result is always a big, bright smile on my mom and dad's faces!

My teachers and friends say that I learn things very quickly. When someone teaches me something new, I usually manage to do it well right away.

Kindness and Helping Others

To me, being a good friend means being kind and helping others when they need it.
Once, my friend fell in the schoolyard, and I immediately helped her
and took her to the nurse so she could feel better. Things like that matter
to me because I want others to be happy.
I also try to be kind to the Earth. I love making useful and practical crafts
from recycled materials to help protect the environment.

My Big Dreams

When I grow up, I don't want to have just one job, I want to be an architect, an artist, and a hairstylist all at once! I want to design houses that are both beautiful and environmentally friendly, homes that use less electricity and have lights that automatically turn off at night, so energy isn't wasted.
I also want to help people in need, for example, by preparing food for them, teaching them useful skills, and, if possible, building homes where they can live safely until they are able to rebuild their own lives.

If I were a superhero and could have supernatural powers, I would want to become invisible, turn into earth or water, and let fire come out of my hands, without burning anything! I'd also love to have the power to make people fly just by snapping my fingers near them, so they could soar into the sky and go wherever I wished. If I were a superhero, another one of my powers would be to fix anything that's broken just by touching it, that way, I could help make everything right again. I'd also team up with my dear cat, Gilbert. Together, we would shrink ourselves and go inside anything dirty, or into the body of any creature that was sick, to destroy the bad germs and gently take care of the good ones. That way, we'd protect nature and help both people and animals stay healthy and live better lives.

I am Pararin, a girl who wants to make the world a little more beautiful through painting, music, creative crafts, new ideas, and, most of all, kindness. Every day I learn, every day I create, and every day I feel more hopeful about the future!

Pararin is a sensitive, perfectionist, and deeply artistic girl. She understands far more than her age might suggest, and in everything she creates, you can see her delicate spirit and rich imagination, in her detailed, colorful drawings, in the pieces she plays on the piano, and in her inventive crafts. She learns very quickly and is now studying music with great enthusiasm and dedication.

You can recognize Pararin's kindness in her everyday behavior. One day, for example, she patiently explained to her brother, Borhan, how to recognize his emotions and respond more calmly. Her warm and respectful way of communicating with others makes her presence soothing in any group. Even in her interactions with animals and nature, she is gentle and considerate.

We feel proud every time we look at Pararin's artwork. One funny thing about her is that she still sometimes calls her blanket (Patoo in Persian) "Tapoo", a sweet keepsake from her early childhood!

In recent years, Pararin's growth in creativity, focus, and discipline has been remarkable. She has the ability to turn her ideas into real projects and approaches everything she does with precision, imagination, and perseverance. We believe these qualities will guide her on her path toward artistic and personal fulfillment.

My Family Says...

Atbin's World

I'm Atbin, and I'm Confident

Hi! My name is Atbin Ramezanpour, and I'm 13 years old.
What I'm most proud of is my self-confidence. I believe in who
I am and what I can do, whether I'm on the soccer field, in the kitchen,
or making music. Hard work and passion are significant parts of who I am,
and I believe they are what make me unique. I always give my best,
and I never give up on something I care about.

My Passions

Soccer is one of my biggest passions. Scoring a goal in a tournament is when I feel the happiest and most confident; it's the moment everything comes together. My friends and teachers appreciate my hard work in soccer, and I do my best to improve my skills, such as perfecting my free kicks so that I never miss them. Soccer isn't the only thing I love, though. Cooking is another activity I could do all day without getting bored. When I'm not in the kitchen or on the field, I'm listening to French rap or creating my own rap songs. Music gives me energy and allows me to express myself in a way that nothing else can.

What Makes Me Special

What makes me special is my mix of self-confidence, hard work, and passion.
I love talking about soccer and rap because they inspire me and
motivate me to move forward. I also believe in being a good friend
by always having my friends' backs.
Family means a lot to me, too; they are the people I care about most.

Making a Difference

I believe that fairness is really important. When I was 10, I saw a friend in school being bullied by older kids, and I stood up for him. That moment showed me the importance of protecting people and fighting against injustice by taking the right, lawful steps. If I could help anyone, it would be those who struggle with self-doubt. I'd give them tips and encouragement to boost their confidence, because I know how much believing in yourself can change your life.

My Big Dreams

When I grow up, I want to be a rapper. My dream isn't just about the music;
it's also about using the money I earn to give to charities and help those in need.
I want to show the goodness of this world and inspire others to never give up.
If I could teach the world one lesson, it would be precisely that: no matter
how hard things get, keep moving forward. If I were a superhero, my power
would be the ability to go back in time. I'd use it to repair my mistakes and
give myself and others a second chance. With that power, I'd try to make
life kinder and better for people who've been hurt or left behind.

I am Atbin, and I believe that even without
superpowers, with confidence, hard work,
and passion, I can make a real difference.

What makes Atbin so special is the balance between his emotional side and his strong, assertive character. He is kind and caring, yet also confident and determined. One of his greatest strengths is his ability to connect with people of different personalities. With his upbeat, energetic vibe, he can start and carry a conversation easily, making everyone around him feel included. His social skills shine not only with his friends of the same age, but also with adults and younger children.

A memory that still touches us is from when he was very young, playing soccer with other kids in a park. A much younger boy, new to the game, was struggling to keep up. Atbin not only played seriously but also looked after him, even stopping the game to tie the boy's shoelaces, at a time when tying laces was not easy for him either. That mix of care and responsibility showed his kind heart.Recently, Atbin has learned how to manage his various emotions better, responding with increased confidence and assertiveness. One of our proudest moments was during his piano tutor's 20th anniversary concert. Ultimately, after playing the piano, he performed a rap song he had written. He practiced hard, faced his nerves, and dared to share something unique. It was unforgettable.

Atbin has been practicing karate since 2019. His dedication, training three times a week including a day in weekends, after school, even during exam periods or when he wasn't feeling well, earned him the prestigious black belt, a milestone that required great perseverance. He now coaches junior karate students once a week while continuing his own training to develop his skills further.At home, Atbin also makes a difference through his cooking. Inspired by new tastes, he taught himself to cook like a professional, even inventing his own sauces. Now, he regularly prepares healthy meals for our family, a responsibility he takes on with pride. Of course, one funny thing about him is how quickly he bursts into laughter; once he starts, he can't stay serious.

My Family Says...

Raha's World

I'm Raha, and in My Drawings, the Trees Laugh!

Hi! My name is Raha Soroush, and I'm five years old. I love drawing; when I make lines on paper with my colored pencils, I feel like I'm telling a story to the world. Sometimes in my drawings, the trees laugh, and the cats sing! I love making puzzles, and when I find the last piece, I get so excited and start laughing. I also really enjoy making crafts. With cardboard and paint, I create new things, sometimes a dollhouse and sometimes a little boat for my bathtub.

Whenever I receive a gift, I jump up and down with excitement, laugh with joy, and tell my family and friends all about it.

I have a good memory and can recall details of what I see or hear. For example, after watching a cartoon just once, I can easily retell the entire story! Many times, I make up new stories for my mom and dad and tell them with excitement. I can remember all the beautiful moments of my life again and again, like my preschool memories, the prizes I've won, the trips I've taken, or even my playtime adventures with friends..

Play and Energy

I love active games! Sometimes I jump up and down on the mat, and sometimes
I stand on my hands, just like gymnasts! When I do it right, everyone claps,
and I feel so happy! Sometimes my mom and I come up with fun active games
and have competitions together. On some days, my dad and I go to the
amusement park. There, I ride the tall slides and laugh all day long!
Playing with my auntie and my friends is also so much fun; we play with water,
build sandcastles or snowmen, and laugh while eating ice cream when we get tired.

Learning and Growing

I try to do things on my own: I dress myself, put away my toys, and when
a problem comes up, I try to think and find a solution by myself.
If I can't, I ask Mom for help. At preschool, I've learned to wait for
my turn and not to say bad words. My teacher says
I'm responsible and always respect other people's turns.
I enjoy preparing food for my pet and spending time playing with it.
When I pet it, I feel calm and happy. I always care about animals
and nature because I know they are alive too and need to be cared for.

I believe kindness means taking care of others. I look after my friends, for example, once when my friend fell, I helped her stand up. Sometimes I collect items I no longer need, such as shoes or toys, to donate to charity, allowing other children to enjoy them. When I do this, my heart feels warm. I also help at home and have learned that kindness means doing small things filled with love.

My Big Dreams

I love to imagine and dream. Sometimes I draw storybooks with imaginary
pictures and tell stories about heroes. When I grow up, I want to have
a toy-making workshop and, next to it, a toy store with a play area.
I want all children to come here to play, run, laugh, learn, and watch cartoons,
especially my favorites like Cocomelon, Sunny Bunnies, and Molang!
If I were a superhero, I'd make sure everyone always laughed, even when
they were sad! I'd love to create amazing things and help people. In my imagination,
I visit beautiful places with my mom or auntie, where I plant flowers,
play games, and make the world a happier place. Maybe if I had magical powers,
I'd take the place of Piu Piu and Molang, do fun things, and solve everyone's problems!.

I am Raha, a girl with a kind heart,
a happy face, and creative hands. I
draw to create smiles, play to spread joy
everywhere, and learn so that
one day I can help everyone be happy.

Raha is a girl with a brilliant mind and a keen eye for the world around her.
She remembers everything in great detail and describes it with sweet,
precise words. Her verbal skills go beyond her age;
when she speaks, she places words together with both feeling and order.
Raha also has remarkable artistic talent, her drawings and
crafts are full of imagination and color, as if she brings
her inner world to life on paper.
Raha is kind and compassionate. Once at preschool, she helped a friend
who had fallen, and another time, she made peace between two classmates
who were upset. She loves nature, too. We have a funny
memory of her that always makes us smile: last spring, whenever
she saw a forest or garden, she planted the fallen branches she found on
the ground, hoping they'd turn into trees. And amazingly,
a few of them actually sprouted! Raha has also made significant
progress recently in coloring with markers and learning English.
We were prouder than ever when she was able to
stay calm and enjoy every moment at her preschool, right then,
we knew our daughter was on the path of growth and blossoming.

My Family Says...

Katayoun's World

I'm Katayoun, and I Notice Every Detail!

Hi! My name is Katayoun Velayati, and I'm 12 years old. One of the things that makes me proud of myself is my memory. I don't just remember ordinary facts or answers; I can recall exact memories, who looked at whom at a party, or even the details from months ago. Remembering those little things helps me narrate events in a way that feels real and vivid.

People often say I'm a great storyteller because I include all the details others might leave out. I also enjoy solving mysteries and imagining how unsolved cases might unfold; it challenges my mind and keeps me curious.

Helping and Lifting Others

I feel happiest when I'm helping younger children, whether I'm teaching them something new or guiding them through their work. Explaining things in a way they can understand makes me feel confident and responsible. If I could teach one skill, it would be how to use details in stories or writings. Descriptive writing brings stories to life, making people imagine the story as it goes. Another skill I've learned over time is how to give good feedback. I try to lift others through my words and actions, helping them feel more positive without even realizing I've done it. That's something I'm proud of, because it means I can use kindness to make a difference.

Inspired by Music and Creativity

When I'm not teaching or storytelling, I spend a lot of time listening to music, especially my favorite K-pop band, Stray Kids. Their songs give me energy and confidence, and I could listen to them all day without getting bored. If I had an entire day to myself, I'd spend it learning all of their dances. It would be fun, give me exercise, and make me feel closer to the music I love. I also love talking about Stray Kids so much that even my teachers know how important they are to me. I've worked on six school projects about their group, and my friends often joke that I could talk about them forever.

Caring about Others

One of the sayings I live by is "treat others how you want to be treated."
To me, being a good friend means noticing when someone's behavior feels
different and making sure they feel safe and supported. I try to check in on people,
ask questions, and give them space to share what they are going through.
Fairness and kindness are very important to me. I believe that everyone deserves
to be treated equally, regardless of their gender, nationality, or background.
I remember once at my taekwondo class on Halloween, a younger kid started
crying because he didn't have enough candy. Since I had more than enough,
I gave him one of my bags and later shared the extra candy I received
with other kids, too. Moments like that remind me of the
importance of spreading kindness.

My Big Dreams

For my future career, I am still unsure about my desired path. I have many ideas, but I struggle to settle on just one. I take many classes to help figure myself out and see which one catches my eye the most. But beyond a career, I want to be someone who treats others with fairness, kindness, and respect. I also want to demonstrate independence and determination, as these qualities enable me and others to move forward.

If I could teach the world one lesson, it would be not to judge people too quickly. You never really know what someone is going through behind the scenes, so paying attention to details and choosing kindness can make a huge difference. If I were a superhero, I would want powers that help me protect and understand others. I'd choose night vision to notice people who are hiding or isolating themselves, and mind-reading so I could understand what people are thinking and feeling. My objective would be to help anyone who feels lonely, misunderstood, or upset feel safe, valued, and confident again.

I am Katayoun, and even though I'm still young, I know that every day I can grow into the person I want to be: thoughtful, fair, kind, and ready to use my voice and creativity to make a difference.

Katayoun is a determined and hardworking girl. Once she sets her mind on something, she gives it her full effort until she achieves it. Alongside that determination, she possesses a very caring personality, continually seeking ways to support others and ensure that the people around her feel included and comfortable. One moment that showed this side of her clearly was during a shopping trip with a friend. Her friend needed larger sizes, so Katayoun chose to buy a bigger size for herself too, just so her friend wouldn't feel bad. That thoughtful choice revealed her kindness and ability to put others before herself. Recently, we've seen real growth in her maturity. She is learning to manage her excitement in a balanced way, celebrating her successes with pride but also with humility. This summer, she joined us in the office most days and worked on developing stronger focus and discipline. Watching her take responsibility and push herself to improve made us proud. At home, she adapts easily, whether helping us with guests or enjoying a movie night together. She connects well with people of all ages, especially younger children and our staff, building warm and lasting relationships. What makes her unique is her mix of maturity and childlike joy. Though she looks older now, she still lights up with pure delight when playing with her favorite doll. That balance makes her truly special.

My Family Says...

Some of our young authors also shared their beautiful artwork...

I'm Raha, and in my drawings, the trees laugh!

Published by North Star Success Inc.

 www.northstarsuccess.com

 support@northstarsuccess.com

 +1 647 479 0790